Growing Up Where Jesus Lived

Third Edition

abeka.
Pensacola, FL 32523-9100
an affiliate of PENSACOLA CHRISTIAN COLLEGE®

W9-CUD-921

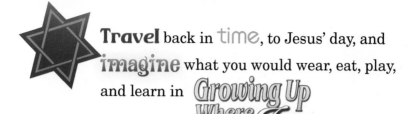

Travel back in time, to Jesus' day, and imagine what you would wear, eat, play, and learn in *Growing Up Where Jesus Lived.*

To Teachers and Parents

From the dusty streets of Nazareth to the Temple in Jerusalem, there is much to learn about ancient Israel. See the world in which Jesus grew up, as students discover the differences between life in the first century and life today. Your student will enjoy discovering the treasure found in God's Word within the Treasure Chest at the back of the reader. He will also be challenged to consider the material and draw conclusions from it with interpretive questions. His imagination will be expanded as he begins to picture what life would be like if he grew up where Jesus lived.

Growing Up Where Jesus Lived
Third Edition

Staff Credits
Authors: Joan Ripley Smith, Juliane Roberts
Managing Editor: Amy Yohe
Edition Editors: Tanya Harrington, Rachel Grosnick, Bethany Roberts
Designer: Michelle Johnson
Production Artist: Susan Schmuck
Illustrators: Jamieson Jekel, John Ball, Matthew Sample II

Credit(s): Cover-malkani/Depositphotos, Inc. (background); icons used throughout-KaterinaMatroskin/iStockphoto.com (jewel), Allevinatis/iStockphoto.com (old map/spyglass), drmakkoy/iStockphoto.com (candle), andegro4ka/iStockphoto.com (scroll); 71-tanys04/iStockphoto.com

Cataloging Data
Smith, Joan Ripley.
    Growing up where Jesus lived / written by Joan Ripley Smith
140 p.: col. ill.; 22 cm. (abeka reading program)
    1. Reading, Elementary. 2. Readers, Elementary. III. Abeka Book, Inc.
Library of Congress: PE1119.S65 G76 2017
Dewey System: 428.6

Contents

Discovering Treasures from the Bible

As we travel through the Mediterranean Sea, past the rocky coast of Greece and the pyramids of Egypt, we come to a small land, dotted with beautiful mountains and sparkling seas. This is Israel. In this country many years ago, Jesus was born. Here He lost His first tooth, went to school, worked hard with Joseph, and performed many amazing miracles.

The Bible calls Jesus the Pearl of Great Price, because Jesus is the greatest treasure found in God's Word. As we walk through the streets of Israel and see how the people lived and served God, we will find other hidden treasures.

When you see a small jewel, this means that there is treasure in the Bible that we need to find. Turn to the treasure chest at the back of the book and look for the numbered jewel that matches the jewel you found. As you read, you will discover many of these hidden treasures along the way.

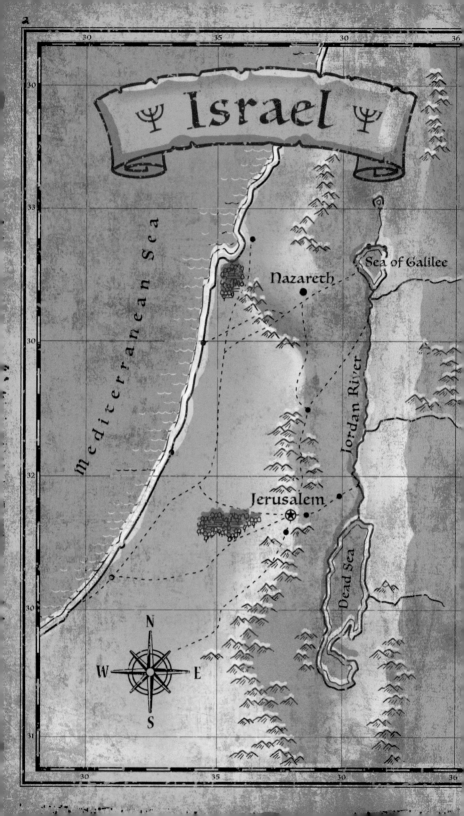

Introduction

A little over two thousand years ago, God sent His Son, Jesus, to live on the earth. The Bible tells us that He came as a newborn baby to a woman named Mary, who was married to a man named Joseph. Mary and Joseph lived in Israel, or the Holy Land.

Israel was a tiny land at the eastern end of the Mediterranean Sea. *Israel* is the name of the country today. Though it was small, the land had all these things: high, snowy mountains and the Dead Sea (the lowest place in the whole world); dry deserts and thick forests;

wild jungles and rocky cliffs with caves; the Mediterranean seashore; a huge lake called the Sea of Galilee; and the Jordan River, which ran through the middle of the land.

Many animals lived in the Holy Land. Donkeys, camels, sheep, and goats could be seen everywhere. And when Jesus lived there, there were many wild animals, too.

Lions, bears, wolves, leopards, hyenas, and wild boars could all be found in that

land. When Jesus was a boy, Israel was a beautiful and interesting place in which to grow up.

Even though He was the Son of God, Jesus lived in the same kind of house, ate the same kind of food, and wore the same kind of clothes as the children who were His neighbors. In this book you will find out what it was like to grow up in Israel the way Jesus did two thousand years ago.

 ## Think About It!

Give the correct answers.

1. How was Jesus the same as other boys and girls?

*2. What made Jesus different from all other children?

Words to Watch For

Nazareth	garbage	lattice
courtyard	laundry	cistern

Chapter *1*

Where Would You Live?

In Israel there were only a few big cities. Jerusalem was the largest one. There were many small towns, though, and even more villages. Jesus lived in one of these tiny villages with His parents and His brothers and sisters. The village was called Nazareth. Only a few hundred people lived there when Jesus was a boy. There were many other villages in Israel that were like Nazareth.

Few wealthy people lived in these small villages. Many of the men were farmers. The farmers were poor, but their families always had plenty of good food to eat.

7

The families lived close together so they could be near the village well. They could also help protect each other from robbers.

Early in the morning, the farmers took their donkeys or oxen to the fields. Sometimes they had to walk a long way. They worked in their fields all day, using the animals to help plow or to carry things. At sunset, the farmers and their animals walked back to the village to be with their families.

The streets in the villages were not paved. After a rain, they would be a muddy mess. In the summer, they were dusty. People dumped their garbage and dirty water in the street. Because of this, there was often a bad smell.

Most of the streets were very narrow. Sometimes,

people had to step into a doorway when a
donkey loaded with bundles passed by.

There were dogs lying in the streets,
but they were not pets. These yellow
wolf-like dogs spent their time sleeping,
barking at each other, and eating the
garbage in the streets. To call a person a
dog was a terrible insult.

The houses on the street were very
plain looking. Most people just thought
of their house as a safe place to sleep and
a place to be protected from the rain and
sun. They stayed outside as much as they
could.

The windows facing the street were
high and covered with thin strips of wood

called *lattice*. From the street, you could not see inside, but the people inside could see out.

Most houses were made of mud bricks or of stones held together with mud. Wealthy people had houses made of stones cut into blocks.

The inside walls of the houses were plastered and covered with white lime to make them look clean. There were no pictures decorating the walls. It was thought that having a picture might tempt someone to worship what was in the picture instead of worshiping God.

In some poor homes, the floor was just pressed mud. It had to be swept every day and sprinkled with water to keep it from getting too dusty. A better floor would be made of lime and pebbles (a mixture like cement) or of slabs of stone fitted together. It would be easy to lose something small in the cracks of this kind of floor. ◄2►

The front door was made of thick wood. Some doors had a heavy iron ring on the outside for a knocker and a lock that was opened with a large key. The windows had shutters that were closed at night.

If you lived in Israel at this time, you would probably not have had special rooms for the bathroom or kitchen. In fact, many families lived in a house that had only one room. They may have kept some animals in the house with them. Sheep, goats, and maybe even a donkey or a cow would sleep in one end of the room, which was a step lower than the rest of the room. If you lived in a home like this, you would be used to the smell and noise. It would be fun to play with the animals. Your parents might

let you make a pet of a baby lamb that lived in your house. Maybe it could even sleep with you.

The roof on most houses was made of mud pressed over some branches or reeds. The branches rested on a few large wooden beams. The mud had to be smoothed out and pressed with a stone roller several times a year. This special roller was usually kept on the roof. Sometimes after a heavy rain, the roof would leak. In the middle of the night you might have to get up and move your bed to a dry place. Since the roof was made of mud, sometimes grass would grow on top of your house.

All houses were supposed to have a low stone wall around the roof so no one would fall off. There were stairs up to the rooftops since people went there often.

Why would you go up to the rooftop? You could store things up there. You could dry raisins and figs there. You could sleep there on a hot night. You could go on the rooftop to

13

see something that was happening in the street. You could go there to study or pray. Since the rooftops sometimes were joined, you could get to a friend's house that way.

In the summer, some people made a little booth out of leaves and branches for sleeping on the rooftop. Others built a room of stone or brick which could be used for a guest room. A wealthy family might build several rooms on the roof. They would call this their summer house, and the house below would be their winter house.

A house with more than one room downstairs would have a courtyard, with the rooms built around it. The courtyard was a place where you could be outdoors but inside the house at the same time. Your courtyard might have a garden of shady trees and flowering bushes.

Sometimes several families shared a courtyard. It would be a busy place. The men would load and unload their donkeys there.

The women might do their laundry or
cooking in the courtyard. It would be fun
to eat a meal there on a sunny day. On a
cold day you could warm your hands over a
fire burning in your courtyard. It would be
a good place to play. You could even take a
bath there!

Some courtyards had a cistern. This was a large rock-lined hole where rainwater was collected. Special drains carried the water from the rooftop to the cistern. You could use that water instead of getting water at the well every day.

Words to Watch For

furniture	containers	storage
parchment	Palestine	

If your family were poor, you wouldn't have much furniture in your house. For sleeping and sitting, you would have only mats made of wool or reeds. At night, the mats were spread out on the floor in a row. Your father would sleep at one end, your mother at the other, and you and your brothers and sisters would sleep in between. ◄3►

Families who weren't poor had wooden beds. Some were big enough for both parents and a few small children, too. They were high, and you would use a footstool to get up into them. Sometimes a cloth was hung above the bed to keep the insects out. There might also be chairs in the house. One kind had three wooden legs and a leather seat. It could be folded up.

At meal time, mats were used instead of chairs. If your family had a wooden table, it would be very low; or your table might be only an animal skin spread out on the ground.

There were some things that every home needed. Every house had lamps. They were usually made of pottery, but they could be metal. Olive oil was poured inside the lamp, and a cloth wick was placed in the oil with the tip sticking up. Then the tip was lit. One lamp was kept burning all night.

The lamps did not burn very brightly. Some lamps had places for several wicks. Even  with one of these lamps burning, your house would still be somewhat dark. At night it would be hard to read or sew.

Every home had many pottery or metal containers. Your family would need these things: large jars to store water, large pitchers to carry water from the well, small pitchers and storage jars for oil, storage jars for grain, cooking pots and pans, a bowl and pitcher for washing hands, a large bowl for washing feet, drinking cups, serving bowls, and a very small bowl to hold salt.

Many homes also had bags to hold liquids that were made of the whole skin of a goat. Large and small baskets were needed to store and carry things. Of course, every home had a broom.

One of the most important things in the home was the grinding mill. It was made of two large, flat, round stones, one put on top of the other. The grains of wheat or barley were put in a hole on the top. It took two people to move the top stone around. They sat across from each other, and both held onto the wooden handle with one hand. As the stone was turned, flour came out from between the stones. The flour was used to make bread.  A small metal box called a *Mezuzah* [mĕ-zoo′zŭ] could be found on the doorpost of many homes. Inside was a folded square of parchment. (Parchment is smooth animal skin, almost like paper.) Special Scripture verses were written on it. As your parents went in and out of the house, they would touch the box, then kiss their fingers. This was to remind them of God and His commandments.

There were some families in Palestine that never lived in a house at all. They lived in tents. The tents were made of black goat's hair. The goat-hair cloth kept the family cool in the summer and dry in

the winter. Curtains were used to make
rooms inside the tent.

Since the tent was moved to different
places, only those things that were really
needed could be taken along. There are still
people today who live in the same kind of
goat-hair tent.

Think About It!

Give the correct answers.

1. Name the village where Jesus lived as a child.

*2. Describe how most houses were made.

What Do YOU Think?

*How do homes in Jesus' day compare to your home today?

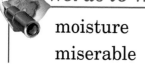
Words to Watch For

moisture	accidentally	heaviest
miserable	unbearably	sirocco

Chapter *2*

What Would the Weather Be Like?

Israel was a land of sunshine and outdoor living. Usually, not one drop of rain would fall from May to September—five whole months! The only moisture during that time was from the dew that came during the night. If you accidentally left something outside overnight, it would be wet with dew in the morning. The dew was good for growing grapes, olives, and figs. **◀6▶**

Finally, in October and November some rain would fall and would soften the hard, dry earth. The heaviest rains came in December, January, and February. It might even snow a little in some high places. March and April brought sunshine and

23

wildflowers. Blooms of all colors covered the hillsides, but the flowers quickly withered when the dry season began again in May.

Refreshing winds often came from the sea in the west, but sometimes hot winds came from the desert in the east and made life miserable. Outside, it was unbearably hot, and sandy dust would blow in your eyes. Inside, it was almost as hot, and even though the shutters on the windows were closed, sand would still get in your food and clothes. There was no place to get away from it. This hot wind still blows in Israel today and is called *sirocco*.

 ## Think About It!

Give the correct answers.

1. How do grapes, olives, and figs grow without rain?

2. In which months is there the most rain?

Chapter *3*

What Would Your Family Be Like?

Your mother and father would have been married at a young age. A girl usually got married at thirteen and a boy at about eighteen.

The boy's parents decided which girl he should marry; then they made an agreement with the girl's parents. (If she was really against marrying a certain person, she could say no.)

After a waiting time of about a year, the wedding would take place. The celebrations lasted a whole week, and afterwards the bride and groom went to live near the man's family or with them.

When children were born, the parents would think of them all as gifts from God. They would be happier, though, if they had a baby boy. This was because in those days, having a big family was important. Daughters got married and moved away, making the family smaller. But sons brought their wives home, and grandchildren were born into the family making it even bigger. So, families celebrated more when a son was born.

The newborn baby was washed, rubbed with salt, and then wrapped tightly in *swaddling clothes.* The swaddling was strips of cloth five or six yards long. The wrapped baby could not move his arms or legs. **7**

When a baby boy was eight days old, he was named at a special ceremony. The first birthday was remembered, but the family usually did not celebrate any more birthdays after the first one.

When the child was about two, there was another party. This was to celebrate the weaning of the child. This meant that the boy or girl no longer had to be nursed by the mother, but could drink from a cup.

A special event took place on a boy's third birthday. It was the day he would get his first haircut. Friends of the parents came over and helped cut the hair.

Girls did not get haircuts. They always let their hair grow long.

Children were taught always to obey their parents. You would give special respect to your father, who was the head over the family. He would lead your mother, you and your brothers and

sisters, and the servants. And when you
had children of your own, he even led them!
Since your grandparents probably would
live in the same house with you, you would
obey them as well as your parents.

If you were a boy, your father would
teach you some kind of work to do. This
was so you could have an honest job when
you grew up. When you were twelve, or
even before, he would probably teach you to
do the same kind of work he did.

You might be a farmer, like many men
in Israel, and grow grain, olives, grapes,
and figs. You might learn to be a carpenter
(Jesus' earthly father was one), a weaver,

a potter, a bricklayer, a fisherman, a
tentmaker, a merchant, a metalsmith, a
stonecutter, a shepherd, a dyer of cloth, or
a tanner (preparer of leather). You might
even be a teacher, a doctor, a musician, or a
banker.

A father's most important
responsibility was to teach his children
about God. About two thousand years

before Jesus was born, there lived a great man named Abraham, who trusted in God. God showed Himself to Abraham in a special way and promised to bless all his family. **8** The family grew and grew, and the people who came from Abraham's family were called "Jews." God gave the Jewish people commandments to follow and taught them His laws when He sent Moses to be their leader. **9** A Jewish father was to carefully teach these very laws to his children.

A father also taught his children about an important promise that was given by God. The promise was that some day God would send a Savior who would be born into the family of Abraham. He would be holy and perfect and would take the punishment for the sins of God's people. This Savior would bless not only the Jews, but all the nations of the world. All Jews waited for this promise to come true.

Your mother would take care of you most of the time when you were small. When you were old enough to talk, she might teach you a Bible verse that was chosen especially for you. She would teach you songs from the book of Psalms in the Bible, other Bible verses, and wise sayings. You would practice them until you could say them without one little mistake!

"A merry heart doeth good like a medicine: but a broken spirit drieth the bones."

If your mother knew how, she would teach you to read and write. The language that most people spoke in Israel was called *Aramaic* [ār-ŭ-mā′ĭk].

Unless there were servants in your house, your mother had very little time to play with you. There was so much work for her to do! She had to grind the flour, bake the bread, and do other cooking. She had to spin and weave the wool to make cloth. Then she had to sew the clothes. She also had to mend and wash the clothes, bring the water from the well, find fuel for the fire, and work in the family's

vegetable garden. Sometimes she helped her husband with his work, and of course, she took care of the children, too. As girls grew up, they learned how to do these jobs from their mothers.

 ## Think About It!

Give the correct answers.

*1. How did boys decide what they wanted to be when they grew up?

2. Name a job a boy could learn to do.

3. What did a girl learn from her mother?

Words to Watch For

generous	valuable	younger
bleached	expensive	important
woven	attached	specially

Chapter *4*

What Would You Wear?

When you got dressed this morning, did you have more than one outfit to choose from? If you lived in Jesus' day, you probably wouldn't have many clothes to choose from. Many people had only one set of clothes to wear. Only the very wealthy would have many things to wear. If you wanted to give a generous gift, you might give someone clothes. They were valuable because it took so much work to make them.

You had to be careful not to get your clothes wet, dirty, or torn, because you might not have anything else to wear. If you had a hole in your robe, your mother would patch it, instead of throwing it away. When you were too big to fit into your clothes, they were given to your younger brother or sister. 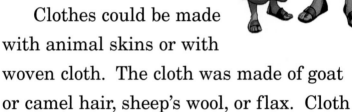 **10**

Clothes could be made with animal skins or with woven cloth. The cloth was made of goat or camel hair, sheep's wool, or flax. Cloth made of goat and camel hair woven together was called *sackcloth*. It was rough and scratchy.

Flax is a plant with blue flowers that has long, stringy fibers in the stem. These fibers can be woven into a cloth

flax

called *linen.* Fine linen, bleached white, was one of the most expensive fabrics. A less expensive linen was made of unbleached flax. Linen was also used for candle wicks.

Most clothes were made from either linen or wool, but Jewish law said the two were not to be mixed together in the same cloth.

If you were a girl, your mother would teach you the important job of spinning and weaving wool. After the wool was taken from the sheep, it had to be washed with soap. Then it was combed, rolled into a rope-like shape, and attached to a spindle. The spindle was a specially shaped stick that would twist the rope into strong, even thread. The thread was then placed on the loom, where it was woven into cloth.

spindle

Cloth could be made fancy by weaving different colors of thread on the loom.

checkered	embroidered	interesting
particular	tunic	shoulder
heaviest	fancier	ashamed

Stripes or even a checkered design could be woven into the cloth. Many women decorated their robes with embroidered designs using a needle and colored thread.

loom

The dyes for coloring the thread came from interesting places. Purple dye (the most expensive) was made from a gland inside a particular sea snail. Red dye could be made from a certain insect. Yellow was made from the yellow crocus flower, and blue came from the indigo plant.

After the cloth was woven, it was sewn into the clothes. Most mothers made the clothing for their whole family, sewing with a big needle made of brass or bone.

Three different kinds of robes were worn in Jesus' time. The first kind was the inner tunic. It resembled a very long shirt without a collar or buttons. It was usually sleeveless and came just below the knee. Some wealthy people wore long tunics down to their ankles. They also had long sleeves.

inner
tunic

Many inner tunics had stripes going down each shoulder, front and back. This tunic was usually the only thing young children wore. Men who worked hard outside would probably only wear a tunic.

At bedtime you wouldn't have to change clothes, because you would wear the same tunic to sleep in.

Most adults wore another layer of clothes over the inner tunic, especially

39

if they were going somewhere outside the house. They could wear another robe called the *coat tunic*. This tunic was a little longer than the inner tunic, and it opened in the front like a coat.

The mantle, or cloak, was the heaviest robe. It was especially important to travelers and shepherds, because it kept them warm during the day and was used for a blanket at night. Many people wore a cloak over their inner tunic for their

coat
tunic

mantle
or cloak

everyday dress. Your mother would have made sure you had a warm cloak to wear in the rainy months.

Girls and women wore the same kinds of robes as men, only theirs were a little longer and fancier. Sometimes a woman's mantle would have a design woven into the corners.

A man's mantle was supposed to have fringes at each of the four corners, with one blue thread in each fringe. The blue thread was to remind him of the Law of God. This was one way to tell the difference between women's clothes and men's. A man would be ashamed to wear a woman's robe.

Your mother might tie little bundles of seeds, herbs, or spices into your robe if you were sick. This was supposed to make you feel better.

overlapped   bracelets   precious
latchets   scorpion   centipede

An important piece of
clothing that was worn with
the inner tunic or coat tunic
was the girdle. It was like
a wide belt, usually made of
linen and wrapped several
times around the waist. You
could keep money, snacks, and
other small things in the folds
of the girdle. You could carry
larger things there as well.

girdle

Sometimes a shepherd might even use his
girdle as a pouch to carry a baby lamb.

If you needed to run or work, you could
tuck the bottom of your tunic into the girdle.
This was called "girding up your loins."

It was important to keep the sun off your
head in very hot weather. Men usually wore
a turban, made of cloth wound around the

head. Sometimes a cloth was worn over the head and also hung down the neck and back. A man did not feel fully dressed without something on his head.

turban

Women wore veils on their heads whenever they went out. They even wore veils in their own house when they had company. Sometimes it was hard to tell who was under the veil if the face was covered. You might not even recognize your own

veil

mother! Jewish women did not always have their whole face covered by a veil. Instead, they hid their face when they saw a man coming.

Women and girls gave much attention to their hair, even though it was usually covered. It was always long. Some ladies braided their hair in several braids or wound their hair around their head in a fancy design. They used combs or even gum to make the hair stay in place. ◀11▶

Men usually kept their beards long and only trimmed them a little to keep them neat. They were very proud of their hair and beard and sometimes put olive oil on them to make them shine.

Women also used olive oil. They put it on their face every day to keep the skin soft. Sometimes it was mixed with expensive perfume and sweet-smelling spices. ◀12▶

Some ladies painted their eyelids with black makeup, using a polished metal mirror to see themselves. Ladies also used red makeup to make their cheeks look rosy.

Women and girls enjoyed wearing jewelry. They could wear earrings, necklaces, anklets, combs, and bracelets. The jewelry could be made of gold, silver, pearls, ivory, precious stones, or glass. Coins were sometimes used in jewelry, too.

The signet ring was a piece of jewelry men wore. A man had his own design on his ring. When he pressed his ring in wax or clay, the design would look like he had signed his name.

signet ring

Many people wore sandals on their feet. They usually were made of leather or wood and were strapped to the feet with strips of leather called *latchets*. You would take off your shoes every time you went inside. The custom was to take off your left sandal first, and put it on last.

If you went barefoot, you would be careful not to step on a scorpion or centipede. They both have painful stings.

Think About It!

Give the correct answers.

1. What type of animal hair or wool was used to make clothing?

2. Where did the dye used for coloring thread come from?

*3. What piece of clothing acted as a pocket?

4. What might a man use in place of signing his name?

cucumbers   dandelions   pomegranates
pistachio   flavored   biscuits
unleavened   Jehovah   refrigerators
lentils: *a vegetable that grows inside of
    a pod just as peas and beans do*

Chapter 5

What Would You Eat?

Many of the foods eaten in Jesus' day
are common foods you may eat today. Most
of your food would have been grown in your
own garden or in the village fields. You
would eat lettuce, cucumbers, dandelions,
melons, pomegranates, beans, lentils, peas,

and onions from your garden. Oranges, dates, walnuts, almonds, and pistachio nuts grew on trees in the land of Israel. Figs and grapes were favorite fruits. They could be eaten fresh in the summer and fall, or they could be dried on the rooftops to be eaten during the winter. Sometimes raisins and figs were pressed together into "cakes." The dried figs could also be strung on a rope and hung in your house until they were needed.

Most of the grapes were squeezed for their juice. The juice had to be strained before it was served, to be sure there weren't any insects or bits of grape. Grape juice was also used to make grape-honey. The juice was boiled until thick and sweet like honey, then eaten on bread.

Bread that was spread with butter and bee's honey was a treat that children especially liked.

Olive oil was used in preparing many foods. You would use it the way we use butter on bread and vegetables. Your mother would also use olive oil in the things she cooked. ◀13▶ The women were very good at making different flavored sauces and using tasty spices.

Meat was not eaten very often. If you lived near the water, you could have fresh fish. Other people ate fish that had been dried and salted so that it would not spoil. For a special meal, you might have goat's meat. A lamb or a calf would only be cooked for the most important celebrations. ◀14▶

Your milk might come from a goat, a sheep, a cow, or a camel! You could drink it fresh, or it could be used to make butter, cheese, or a food that looked like lumpy yogurt.

Bread was the most important food in Israel. It was eaten at every meal. Bread was never cut with a knife but had to be broken into pieces with your hands. When you "broke bread," it meant that you had eaten a meal. Bread could be made of barley or wheat flour. It could be baked into big, round loaves that looked like stones, small biscuits, or paper-thin pancakes. Bread could be made into fancy cakes with seeds, nuts, honey, or grape-honey. Flat, heavy bread made without yeast, or leaven, was called *unleavened bread*.

The bread could be baked in the big town oven or at home. Your mother might have an oven that looked like a big pottery jar. There was a hole at the bottom to build a fire. She placed the bread in through the hole at the top, and the loaves would bake on shelves inside the oven.

Breakfast and lunch were more like snacks than meals. You would have bread, of course, and perhaps some fruit or olives and cheese or dried fish.

For cooking the evening meal, your mother could put her pots right over a fire,

or she might have a clay stove. The clay
stove would have a hole near the bottom
where the fire was built and holes on the
top to rest the pots.

Your mother would have stone
measuring cups, frying pans, large stew

pots, and casserole dishes with lids that fit perfectly. All her pots would be black on the bottom from the fire and smoke. Some homes had a special jar for boiling water. Hot coals were poured into a hole at the bottom, and the water was heated in the top part of the jar.

Your mother would get out pots and pans in the afternoon so she could cook a hot meal to serve after sunset. She might make vegetable stew, lentils, or cooked fish for dinner.

Before eating, everyone had to wash his hands in a special way. You would hold your hands over a wide bowl while someone else poured water over them. There might be a place on the bowl to keep a piece of olive-oil soap and a special place at the bottom where the dirty water drained. A towel for drying was placed on your shoulder.

Also before eating, your family would give thanks to God. This is probably what the prayer would be like: "Blessed art thou, Jehovah our God, King of the world, who causes bread to come forth from the earth." Everyone would say "Amen" at the end. ◀15▶

The men and boys ate first. The women and girls served them and then ate what was left. You would sit on the floor during the meal. Some bread and perhaps a colored glass would be at your place. (Only the wealthy bought expensive clear glass.) You would not use knives, forks, spoons, or plates. How could you eat the food? If it wasn't too juicy, you could pick up pieces with your fingers. The bread was used to scoop up gravies and sauces. Everyone ate the food right from the serving bowl.

If you were a guest at someone's house, the father might take a piece of bread that had been dipped into the food, or a piece of meat, and place it into your mouth. This bite of food was called a sop. It was given to show friendship. **16**

After eating, the family would say another prayer of thanks. Then you would

wash your hands again the same way as before the meal, because they would be dirty! All of the cooked food was usually eaten, but if there were leftovers, they were thrown to the dogs. There were no refrigerators to keep the food from spoiling.

What Do YOU Think?

*Compare eating a meal today to eating a meal in Jesus' day. How is it alike? What is different?

balanced sieve poisonous vineyards
graze: *to eat grass*
cloak: *a coat*

Chapter **6**

What Kinds of Chores Would You Have?

There were some chores that had to be done every day. Every day children helped find things to burn in the fire. It was hard to find enough sticks. Sometimes dried grass, flowers, or thorns had to be used.

If you were a girl, you would learn how to get water from the well. Every evening you would take a big pottery pitcher, a leather bucket, and a rope with you to the well. You would tie the rope to the leather bucket and let the bucket down into the water. After the bucket was drawn back up, you would pour the water into the pitcher. ◄**17**►

Then the full pitcher had to be balanced on your head, shoulder, or hip. Girls sometimes used padding if they were going to carry the pitcher on their head. The pitcher was heavy and would easily break. Sometimes girls came home without water, because their pitcher had broken.

Your mother might ask you to get some embers to help start the fire for cooking dinner. You would take a piece of broken pottery and go to the village baker. The old ashes were raked out of his oven in the evening. He would give you some burnt pieces of wood that were still glowing, and you would carry them home carefully in your piece of pottery.

Sifting the grain was another chore that children could help with. You would put the grain into a sieve, which looked like a basket with holes in the bottom. As you shook the sieve, the good grain fell down through the holes. The straw (chaff) would stay on top as well as pebbles and poisonous seeds. The good grain was washed and spread out on a sheet to dry, usually on the rooftop. The dried grain was then kept in large pottery containers.

If you were a boy, you might have the job of a shepherd and watch the family sheep. You would take the sheep to safe places to eat and drink, and you would protect them from thieves and wild animals. Sometimes girls had the job of watching a flock of goats.

If your mother was making butter, she would probably ask you to help. She would pour milk into a goatskin bag. Then she would hang it from branches or poles. Your job would be to jiggle, shake, and poke the bag until the milk turned into butter.

Grape picking was more like a party than everyday work. When the grapes were ready to pick in September, families

moved into tents or leafy huts near the
vineyards. Men, women, and children
gathered the grapes into baskets. The
workers liked to sing while they picked.

After picking the grapes, the children
could also help make them into juice. The
grapes were put into what looked like
a small wading pool carved out of rock.
Below was a smaller pool, where the juice
drained. Everyone walked around in the

pool, smashing the grapes with their feet. You would sing and clap to the music while you smashed, being careful not to fall. Your feet and legs would be purple for a long time afterward, but it still would be fun.

Another fun job was picking olives. In November, your whole family would go with baskets to collect the ripe olives from

the trees. The olives that had fallen to the ground were picked up first; then the branches were shaken or beaten with a stick until the rest of the olives fell down. Most of the olives were pressed with heavy weights to make oil.

Master Teacher and Good Shepherd

When Jesus lived here on Earth, he did many things. He was a carpenter with Joseph, a shepherd to his disciples, and a master teacher throughout Israel. He could take the simple job of a shepherd and tell a story about His love for everyone. One story Jesus told was about the Good Shepherd. [18] Men have realized that the Good Shepherd is Jesus. When men retell this story they want everyone to know what a wonderful shepherd He is. The story has been retold for over two thousand years.

You may have heard it told like this:

There was once a shepherd who had a flock of one hundred sheep to care for. Some of the sheep were tiny baby lambs with such weak legs that the shepherd had to carry them over the rough places in the road. The shepherd was always kind and good to his sheep.

Each morning he opened the sheepfold and led the flock over the mountain roads and beyond the hills to a wonderful green pasture. In this pasture the sun shone brighter, and the grass grew thicker, and the

brook ran clearer than anywhere else. All day the sheep grazed, drank from the brook, and lay under the shade of the olive trees. The little lambs played in the sunshine with no fear. The shepherd was always quite close by to keep away the wild beasts that hid in the mountain passes. When night came he led the sheep home and kept watch while they slept in the fold.

But one evening as the shepherd entered the fold, something was different. He called softly to the sheep, each one by its name, for he knew them all.

"Aren't my sheep all here?" said the shepherd to himself. Then he went up and down the path, touching each one gently and counting: "One, two, three—" But there were only ninety-nine sheep in the flock. A little lamb was lost!

So the shepherd turned back, leaving the ninety-nine sheep in the

fold. He hurried through the dark
to find the lamb that was lost. He
was a good shepherd. He knew that
he could never leave even one of the
sheep outside.

The stones and the branches
caught at his feet, but on and on he
went, up the mountainside, looking
under every bush and in every
hollow for the little lamb.

At last, when he had gone a long,
long way, he found the little lamb.

It was caught in some bushes by the side of the road. The lamb was crying because one of its legs was cut and bleeding. When the shepherd found it, he laid it tenderly on his shoulders and covered it with his warm cloak. And he went on his way, rejoicing.

The shepherd carried the little lamb all the way back to the fold. The little lamb was tired and sore when they reached home, but he was safe in the arms of the shepherd. The good shepherd called his friends and neighbors, saying to them, "Rejoice with me, for I have found my sheep which was lost!"

John 10:11

"I am the good shepherd: the good shepherd giveth his life for the sheep."

 # Think About It!

Give the correct answers.

1. How many sheep were in the shepherd's flock?

2. How did the shepherd know that a lamb was missing?

3. What did the shepherd do when He returned with the lost sheep?

4. Who is our Good Shepherd?

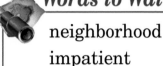

Words to Watch For

neighborhood   Testament

impatient

Chapter 7

What Would School Be Like?

In Jesus' day, only boys needed to go to school. They began school when they were about six. School was held in the neighborhood synagogue [sĭn′ŭ-gŏg], which was like a church.

There were about twenty-five boys in each class. The teacher sat on a stool, the older students on a low bench, and the younger ones sat on mats on the floor.

The Old Testament, part of the Bible, was the only book that the boys used until they were ten years old. The Old Testament was written on rolled-up scrolls in the Hebrew language. Since the children spoke Aramaic at home, they had to learn Hebrew before 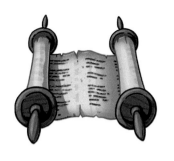 they could read the Old Testament. After studying the Scriptures, the older boys would learn the Jewish laws that were not in the Old Testament.

At the age of twelve or thirteen, most boys finished school.

The main way of learning was to memorize by repeating out loud what the teacher said. People walking by the synagogue could hear the boys' voices, and the parents would know that their children were learning.

The teachers wrote on little wooden boards that were covered with wax. They drew letters on the wax with a pointed stick, and when the board was full, they smoothed out the wax and wrote on the boards again.

A boy might have his own little scroll with a few verses written on it. He could take this home to study.

Boys went to school every day of the week, but on Saturday, the day of rest, they only reviewed their lessons. They went to school two times every day, once early in the morning, and then later in the afternoon. Between ten in the morning and three in the afternoon there was no school because that was the hottest part of the day. Here are some rules a teacher was supposed to follow:

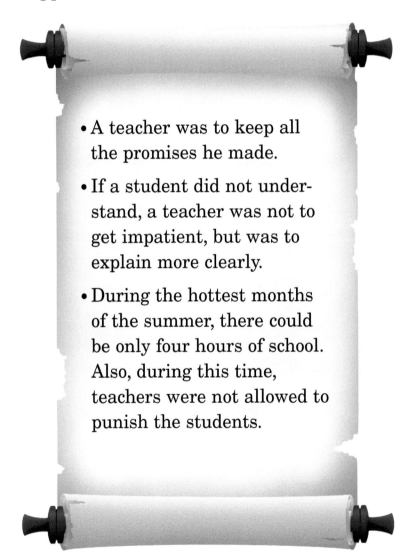

- A teacher was to keep all the promises he made.

- If a student did not understand, a teacher was not to get impatient, but was to explain more clearly.

- During the hottest months of the summer, there could be only four hours of school. Also, during this time, teachers were not allowed to punish the students.

Think About It!

Give the correct answers.

1. Who went to school in Jesus' day?

2. What age were the students who went to school?

3. What were they taught?

*4. Why were students taught the Hebrew language?

Words to Watch For

Chapter *8*

What Would You Do for Fun?

Children were expected to do their share of work around the home, but there was always some time for play. Here are some things you might have done for fun:

• You could gather wildflowers on the hills in the spring.

• You could go swimming. (Most parents taught their children to swim.)

- If you had a hook and string, you could go fishing.
- You might go to the marketplace to look around or meet friends.
- You and your friends could play games with a leather ball stuffed with bran.
- You could play with a pet bird.
- If you lived near a main road, it would be fun to watch groups of travelers on their camels and donkeys. (A group of people traveling together was called a *caravan*. A large caravan could be 200 camels long. Jesus lived near one of these caravan roads.)
- You could make music with a whistle or a flute.
- You could practice hitting a target with your sling shot. **19**
- You and your friends might make up and guess riddles.
- You could look for buried treasure.

(People in the Holy Land sometimes buried their money to keep it safe. Once in a while, the owner would not return to uncover it.)

- You might pretend to be grown up and have a wedding or a funeral.
- You could play with toys. Very young children had clay rattles of different shapes, perhaps a doll or a bird. Some girls had doll houses, complete with small clay pots and pans, clay furniture, and clay dolls. Some of the dolls could even move their arms and legs.

What Do YOU Think?
*Which of these games do you still play for fun?

Words to Watch For

Pharisees   wounded   Samaritan
Preparation   Scriptures   Tabernacles
Pentecost   Pharaoh

religious: *showing or acting as if you*
believe in God

Chapter **9**

How Would You Worship God?

When a boy turned thirteen, he was
thought to be a man. Before his birthday,
he had to learn by heart twenty special
verses from the Old Testament.[20] These
verses were called the *Shema* (shmaw).
All men were supposed to say the Shema
in the morning before they ate and before
they did any work. They also said the
Shema every evening. Before doing
this, a man had to wash his hands and

face. Then he placed his mantle over his head. He also strapped boxes called *phylacteries* [fĭ-lăk′ter-ēz] onto his forehead and his left arm. Inside these leather boxes were Scripture verses to remind men to keep God's laws.

There were some men who wore their phylacteries all the time. Their phylacteries were very big, and the fringes on their mantles were very long. These men were called *Pharisees.* They felt that they were very holy, and they liked to make up laws for everyone to follow. Jesus said that they were not holy, but were proud showoffs.

One of God's commandments was that the seventh day should be a day of rest. The Jews counted Saturday as the seventh day and called it the *Sabbath* (meaning "rest"). The Sabbath began on Friday evening after sunset and lasted until the sun went down on Saturday.

On this day, no one could work. The Pharisees made many rules about what was work and what was not. One rule said that you could only walk a short distance on the Sabbath. Another rule said that a lady could not look in the mirror on the Sabbath because she might see a gray hair and pull it out. That would be considered work.

When Jesus lived on earth, He told a story about proud religious leaders. This story compares the kindness of a stranger to the pride of a priest and a Levite. [21] It is a favorite story that has been repeated for over two thousand years. Here is an example of the story men retold:

There once was a man who was traveling down a lonely road. There were rocks and caves beside this road, where robbers would hide.

All at once, some thieves came out of the place where they had been hiding. They leaped on the man, took away his money and clothes, and left him alone to die.

After a while, a man who was traveling along the road came to the place where the wounded man lay. This man was a priest; he used to stay at the Temple and tell people to be good and kind to each other.

But he was not good and kind himself, for he would not even take the trouble to help the wounded man. Instead of doing so, he crossed over to the other side of the road and pretended that he did not see him.

Soon, another religious
man called a Levite passed by,
but he did not help the wounded man,
either. He walked on, just as the priest
had done, and left him lying on the
ground.

After these two cruel men had
left, another man came along who was
called a Samaritan. As soon as he saw
the wounded man lying in the road, he
stopped, got off his donkey, and went to
him.

The Samaritan felt sorry for the
wounded man, and he did all he could
to help. He poured oil on the wounds

and then bandaged them. He
carefully placed the man on his own
donkey. Then he led the donkey to
an inn, or hotel.

"Take care of him," he said to the
innkeeper. "Here is some money. If
you need any more, I will pay you
when I come again."

Think About It!

Give the correct answers.

*1. Who looked religious on the outside?

*2. Whose actions showed they believed
God's commands?

The Day of Preparation

Friday was called the *Day of Preparation*. Around three o'clock in the afternoon, the women began to prepare the food for the Sabbath, because no cooking could be done after the sun went down. The men did all the chores that needed to be done, so that they could rest the next day. Everyone washed and dressed in their best clothes. A special Sabbath lamp was lit when the sun went down, and the family ate their Sabbath dinner. The food might be cold, but it was the best meal of the week.

Early Saturday morning, the whole family went to the synagogue. The men would be sure to wash their hands and feet before they entered the building. There were places with water near the synagogue where a man could do this, and there might even be a place nearby to take a bath.

As you walked into the synagogue, you would see on both sides of the room sets of long stone benches that looked like wide

stairways. If you sat on the top bench, you
could see everything in the synagogue. At
the far end was a carved chest called an
ark, which held the rolled-up scrolls of the
Old Testament Scriptures. A lamp which
was always lit hung above it. There were
many lamps and candlesticks in the room.
A candlestick with seven branches could
always be found in a Jewish synagogue.

In the middle of the synagogue was a raised platform. On top of that was a pulpit. The reader of the Scriptures would lay the scrolls there while he read.

Every week in the synagogue, the Old Testament was read. After several men took turns reading, a man who had been chosen that week would explain the meaning of the Scriptures. There would also be many prayers and blessings. The service ended just before lunch time. 22

Your family would celebrate many holidays and feasts every year. There was a celebration every month, when a new moon appeared in the night sky. Bonfires were lit on the hilltops to let everyone know when the moon was first seen.

The three most important feasts were the Feast of Tabernacles, Passover, and the Feast of Pentecost. If you lived close to Jerusalem, your whole family might go there for all three feasts, because the Temple of the Jews was there.

Tabernacle means "dwelling place."
The Feast of Tabernacles was celebrated
to remind the Jewish people that their
ancestors lived in tents in the desert. It
was a happy time for all. Your family would
build a booth outside, perhaps in the garden.
The booth would be made of a stick frame
covered with leafy branches. Everyone in
the family would camp out there for a week.

The Feast of Tabernacles was celebrated in the fall, after all the figs, grapes, and olives had been harvested. Thanks was given to God, and the people prayed for enough rain to fall in the coming year. During the feast week, those who came to the Temple to worship (including children) carried branches of palm and other trees, and waved them during the singing of the Psalms.

Passover was another time for remembering the past. The first Passover was in Egypt, where God's people were slaves. God had promised to free them and bring them to a land of their own (Israel), but the Pharaoh (king) of Egypt would not let them go.

This is what God did. He told Moses to tell his people to put the blood of a perfect male lamb on the doorposts of their house, then to roast the lamb and eat it with unleavened bread and bitter herbs. Later that night, the LORD passed over all

the homes in Egypt. He passed over the houses with blood on the doorposts, but inside the houses without the blood, the firstborn child died. Then Pharaoh let God's people go. ◆23◆

The Passover feast was held every year in April. Everyone who could, went to Jerusalem for the week of Passover.

Pentecost (also called the "Feast of Weeks") was always held fifty days after Passover. The Pentecost celebration was held when all the barley and wheat had been harvested. No one worked on the day of celebration. Two special loaves of new, wheat bread were given to God at the Temple. The men brought offerings of the best grain from their crops to thank the Lord for His goodness. **‹24›**

Think About It!

Give the correct answers.

*1. Name the Jewish day of worship?

*2. Why do the Jews celebrate Passover?

3. What feast was held fifty days after Passover?

Words to Watch For

| Joshua | Reuben | Rebekah |
| Esther | generous | |

Chapter *10*

The Passover Visit to Jerusalem

The trip to Jerusalem for Passover was an exciting adventure for Jewish children. **25**
Here is a fictional story of a boy named Joshua and his first visit to Jerusalem:

Joshua was hot, tired, and dusty as he walked up the Mount of Olives, the last hill on the road to Jerusalem. He had been walking uphill all day. Five days ago he had left Nazareth in a large caravan which included his parents and his Uncle Reuben and Aunt Rebekah. His younger sister, Esther, had stayed home with Grandmother.

The roads were dusty, uneven, and full of rocks. Since he was nine years old, Joshua was too big to ride in a box strapped to the side of a donkey like some of the smaller children. It was fun, though, to walk along with so many friends and relatives. Sometimes everyone sang Psalms together as they hiked.

When Joshua came to the top of the hill, he got his first look at the great city of Jerusalem. The tops of hundreds of buildings could be seen behind the walls of the city.

As they walked down the hill, he saw beautiful homes, well-kept gardens, and people setting up tents.

"I'm glad we don't have to spend Passover in a tent, Father," said Joshua.

"Yes, it was very kind of our friends in Jerusalem to invite us to stay in their home," answered his father. "The townspeople are very generous in that way, but there is not enough room in the city for all the visitors."

Words to Watch For

gigantic	magnificent	Antonia
palace	statues	chariots

When the caravan got near the city
wall, Joshua saw that some of the stones in
the wall were gigantic. "This strong wall
was built to protect the city," Uncle Reuben
explained. "You can get inside only through

one of the gates. They are made of thick wood, covered with metal, so that they will be strong enough to keep enemies out. Did you notice that each gate has a tower for the watchman?"

"Don't we need to hurry?" asked Joshua. "The gates will be closed at sunset."

Father explained, "Even if the gates were closed, we could still get inside, Joshua." "Each gate has a small door cut into it, big enough for a man to pass through. The gatekeeper would open it for you. But since it is safer to be inside the city after dark, we had better hurry."

After walking through the gate, Joshua noticed that he was standing in a stone hallway. It was shady and cool there, and there were benches to sit on. The city he had heard so many stories about was just a few steps away.

The streets, which were neatly paved with large, flat stones, led Joshua and his family by the most magnificent buildings he had ever seen.

To Joshua, the huge fortress of Antonia, where the Roman soldiers stayed, looked like a whole town itself. He could imagine being in one of the four giant towers and looking down upon the whole city of Jerusalem.

Then they passed the grand palace of Herod, who had been a ruler in Israel. "I've heard," remarked Joshua's mother, "that the guest rooms in the palace are so large that one hundred people can sleep in each room! Wouldn't it be fun to see all the covered porches, the walkways, the canals filled with water, and the courtyards full of trees and flowers? And, oh yes, those statues that spout water! Can you imagine?"

As he walked through the city, Joshua saw many other wonderful palaces, high towers, large meeting places, and synagogues decorated with carved stone. But for him, the most amazing sight in all Jerusalem was the beautiful Temple of the Jews. It rose high above the city on a huge stone platform. The top part of the Temple shone so brightly that it almost made Joshua's eyes hurt. He couldn't wait to visit there.

It seemed to Joshua that the city was alive with people. He admired wealthy men and women wearing robes with gold threads woven into them and mantles trimmed with fur. He saw Roman soldiers with their swords standing alongside Pharisees praying on the street corners. The sight of the sick begging for food and the slaves being brought to the marketplace made Joshua sad. The streets were crowded with strangers from far countries, and visitors from all over Israel

who had come, like himself, into Jerusalem
for the Passover.

Horse-drawn chariots carrying people were
passing through the streets. Donkeys were
pulling carts packed with things to sell. Those
without horses or donkeys were carrying huge
bundles on their backs. Everyone seemed
to be going to the marketplace just ahead.
When they got there, Joshua was amazed.
"I've never seen things like this in the market
at Nazareth!" he exclaimed. "You could buy
anything you needed here!"

"Yes, and even things you didn't need!"
laughed his mother.

In the market Joshua saw glass from Sidon, fine fabrics from Babylonia and India, and gold from Arabia. Precious stones and expensive jewelry caught Joshua's eye, and the rare perfumes, spices, and ointments smelled wonderful. The sellers made a great deal of noise as they shouted to all who passed, "My goods are the finest you can buy!"

Joshua's family found their friend's house in a quiet part of the city, away from the busy marketplace. The gate at the street was very plain. His father knocked at the door. A servant came to the gate and asked, "Who?" Joshua's father answered only, "I." Since his voice was recognized as a friend's, the servant let everyone into the passageway and led them to the front room. Joshua remembered to take off his sandals before he went in.

The inside of the house looked like no home Joshua had ever seen in Nazareth. On the floor was a design made of hundreds of tiny different-colored tiles. On the ceiling were wood panels carved with more designs. There were also lines and squares painted on the walls. There were some large chairs with backs, couches you could lie down on, and heavy curtains at the sides of the window. Through the window he could see the courtyard. It was paved with marble and planted with palm, pomegranate, and evergreen trees.

The owners of the house came into the room. They were glad to see Joshua's family. "Peace to you, Simeon," the man said, "and to your family." Then he kissed Joshua's father on both cheeks.

"And peace to you," replied Joshua's father. The man spoke to the servant in a low voice, and the servant left. Soon the man's wife brought glasses of cool water for everyone. The drinking glasses were made of perfectly clear glass, and Joshua's mother remarked how lovely they were. Joshua was very careful with his glass.

The servant came back carrying a large copper bowl, a pitcher of water, and some towels on his shoulder. One by one, he washed and dried each person's feet. The cool water felt good on Joshua's hot feet. **26**

That night, preparations for the Passover began. The father of the home lit a candle, and without saying one word looked throughout the house for leaven (the yeast used in making bread). It all had to be thrown out, and only unleavened bread could be eaten at Passover and a whole week afterward.

The blowing of the Temple trumpets woke Joshua the next morning. There would be many things to do, because Passover was that night. The women had to see that the food was bought and prepared. Joshua's mother made sure the family's clothing was clean and mended for the feast. She had made Joshua a new robe that he would wear for the first time at Passover. Everyone took a bath that day in a special room in the house that had a built-in bathtub!

The men had an important job to do. They needed to go to the Temple to sacrifice the Passover lamb, which had been kept outside in a pen. It was a perfectly white male lamb, less than a year old. Joshua's father told him he could help take the lamb to the Temple.

The Temple was bigger and more beautiful than Joshua had ever imagined. ◆27▷ As they climbed the stairs leading up to the Temple, he could look down and see the streets of the lower city. He noticed that most of the people going to the Temple were wearing clean, white robes. Before entering, everyone took off their sandals. Inside, Joshua saw the huge Court of the Gentiles. (*Gentile* means one who is not a Jew. Everyone could go into the Court of the Gentiles.) The ground was paved with marble of different colors. At the sides were porches with tall, white marble columns. Joshua watched the men in the porches selling animals for sacrifice and men changing the money of different countries into the money of the Temple. ◆28▷

Only Jews could go into the middle part of the Temple. After Joshua and his father and uncle climbed the stairs to this part, they passed through a giant brass gate. "This is called the *Beautiful Gate*," explained Uncle Reuben. "It's so heavy that it takes twenty men to open it!" ◀29▶

Once through the gate, they were in the Women's Court. It was called that because women could go no further into the Temple. Joshua stayed there and waited while the men took the lamb up some curved steps and further inside. While he was waiting, he listened to a group of men and children sing Psalms on the steps. Some other men were playing musical instruments.

Joshua could see the smoke from the fat of the lambs being burned on the altar inside. He knew that the blood had been sprinkled on the altar and that the meat was to be taken home and cooked for the Passover feast.

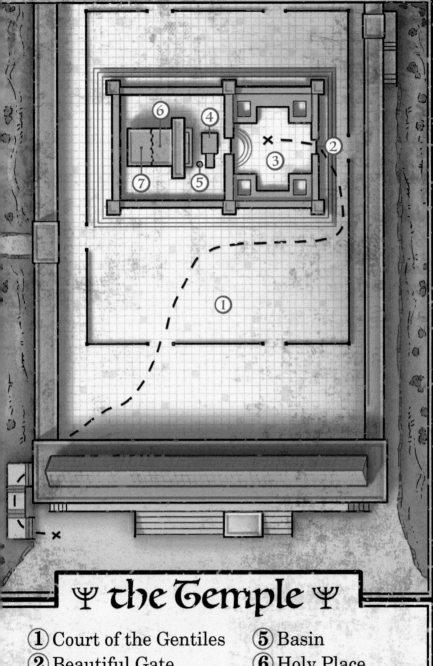

ψ the Temple ψ

1. Court of the Gentiles
2. Beautiful Gate
3. Women's Court
4. Altar
5. Basin
6. Holy Place
7. Holy of Holies

When his father and uncle returned, they told Joshua what they had seen inside: a big stone altar, a huge brass bowl on the backs of twelve lions (used by the priests for washing), and the Holy Place made of giant white marble stones covered with gold.

"Do you remember me telling you about the Holy of Holies, Joshua?" asked his father. "It's inside the Holy Place, behind a thick curtain. Only the High Priest can go in there once a year." **‹30›**

That evening, Joshua's family and friends gathered in the banquet room of the house, wearing their finest clothes. They gave thanks to God, and the feast began. The men lay down on special banquet couches for the ceremonial feast. Each different food was eaten at a special time, with prayers, hymns, and washing of hands in between. This is what the women served: the lamb, which had been roasted whole; unleavened bread; bitter herbs; and a sauce made with vinegar, raisins, and dates.

It was late when everyone was finished eating. Incense was placed on the hot coals of a burner, and Joshua suddenly felt sleepy as the spicy smell of cinnamon filled the room. He was tired, but happy to be included for the first time in the Passover feast at Jerusalem.

The last Passover feast that Jesus ate with His disciples was a very special one. We call it the *Last Supper*. It took place the night before Jesus died on the cross. When the unleavened bread and the fruit of the vine were served, Jesus said they were like His body and blood. He knew that He would be hung on the cross the next day. Jesus also knew that He would come back to life after three days and that He could give eternal life to all those who believed in Him. By dying, Jesus took the punishment for the sins of the whole world. Those who believe will live forever with God in Heaven.

When we have the Lord's Supper (or communion) at church, we think of the death of Jesus and what it means for us. This is what we celebrate instead of Passover, because now Jesus is our perfect Passover Lamb.

 **Think About It!**

Give the correct answers.

*1. What building in Jerusalem impressed Joshua the most?

2. What was the first part of the Temple called?

3. Who is the only person that could go into the Holy of Holies?

*4. Why do we celebrate the Lord's Supper instead of the Passover?

Many things have changed in the world in the last 2,000 years. But the most important change is that the Savior that God had promised has come and has made a way for us to live forever with Him. We read about the Savior Jesus Christ in the Bible.

immediately his feet and ankle bones received strength.

8 And he leaping up stood, and walked, and entered with them into the temple, walking, and leaping, and praising God.

9 And all the people saw him walking and praising God:

10 And they knew that it was he which sat for alms at the Beautiful gate of the temple: and they were filled with wonder and amazement at that which had happened unto him.

11 And as the lame man which was healed held Peter and John, all the people ran together unto them in the porch that is called Solomon's, greatly wondering.

30 Find out what happened to this curtain (veil) on the day that Jesus died on the cross: *Matthew 27:51.*

51 And, behold, the veil of the temple was rent in twain from the top to the bottom; and the earth did quake, and the rocks rent.

temple, and overthrew the tables of the moneychangers, and the seats of them that sold doves.

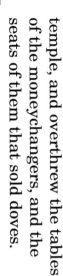

29 After Jesus returned to Heaven, Peter and John attracted a big crowd when they did a miracle at this gate in *Acts 3:1–11.*

1 Now Peter and John went up together into the temple at the hour of prayer, being the ninth hour.

2 And a certain man lame from his mother's womb was carried, whom they laid daily at the gate of the temple which is called Beautiful, to ask alms of them that entered into the temple;

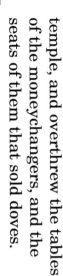

109

3 Who seeing Peter and John about to go into the temple asked an alms.

4 And Peter, fastening his eyes upon him with John, said, Look on us.

5 And he gave heed unto them, expecting to receive something of them.

6 Then Peter said, Silver and gold have I none; but such as I have give I thee: In the name of Jesus Christ of Nazareth rise up and walk.

7 And he took him by the right hand, and lifted him up: and

hands, and that he was come from God, and went to God;

4 He riseth from supper, and laid aside his garments; and took a towel, and girded himself.

5 After that he poureth water into a bason, and began to wash the disciples' feet, and to wipe them with the towel wherewith he was girded.

27 Jesus told His disciples what would happen to that beautiful Temple in *Mark 13:1* and *2.* A few years later it did come true, just as Jesus said.

1 And as he went out of the temple, one of his disciples saith unto him, Master, see what manner of stones and what buildings are here!

2 And Jesus answering said unto him, Seest thou these great buildings? there shall not be left one stone upon another, that shall not be thrown down.

28 It made Jesus angry to see men selling things in the Temple, the place for worshiping God. Read *Matthew 21:12* to see what He did about it.

12 And Jesus went into the temple of God, and cast out all them that sold and bought in the

45 And when they found him not, they turned back again to Jerusalem, seeking him.

46 And it came to pass, that after three days they found him in the temple, sitting in the midst of the doctors, both hearing them, and asking them questions.

47 And all that heard him were astonished at his understanding and answers.

48 And when they saw him, they were amazed: and his mother said unto him, Son, why hast thou thus dealt with us? behold, thy father and I have sought thee sorrowing.

49 And he said unto them, How is it that ye sought me? wist ye not that I must be about my Father's business?

50 And they understood not the saying which he spake unto them.

51 And he went down with them, and came to Nazareth, and was subject unto them: but his mother kept all these sayings in her heart.

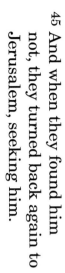 26 A servant quite often did this job, but notice who did the foot-washing in *John 13:3–5.*

3 Jesus knowing that the Father had given all things into his

19 And I will shew wonders in heaven above, and signs in the earth beneath; blood, and fire, and vapour of smoke:

20 The sun shall be turned into darkness, and the moon into blood, before the great and notable day of the Lord come:

21 And it shall come to pass, that whosoever shall call on the name of the Lord shall be saved.

25 Jesus went to Jerusalem when He was twelve. His family thought He had gotten lost there. Read *Luke 2:41-51* to find out where He was found.

41 Now his parents went to Jerusalem every year at the feast of the passover.

42 And when he was twelve years old, they went up to Jerusalem after the custom of the feast.

43 And when they had fulfilled the days, as they returned, the child Jesus tarried behind in Jerusalem; and Joseph and his mother knew not of it.

44 But they, supposing him to have been in the company, went a day's journey; and they sought him among their kinsfolk and acquaintance.

5 And there were dwelling at Jerusalem Jews, devout men, out of every nation under heaven.

6 Now when this was noised abroad, the multitude came together, and were confounded, because that every man heard them speak in his own language.

7 And they were all amazed and marvelled, saying one to another, Behold, are not all these which speak Galilaeans?

8 And how hear we every man in our own tongue, wherein we were born? . . .

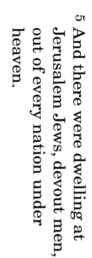

12 And they were all amazed, and were in doubt, saying one to another, What meaneth this? . . .

16 But this is that which was spoken by the prophet Joel;

17 And it shall come to pass in the last days, saith God, I will pour out of my Spirit upon all flesh: and your sons and your daughters shall prophesy, and your young men shall see visions, and your old men shall dream dreams:

18 And on my servants and on my handmaidens I will pour out in those days of my Spirit; and they shall prophesy:

they were thrust out of Egypt, and could not tarry, neither had they prepared for themselves any victual.

40 Now the sojourning of the children of Israel, who dwelt in Egypt, was four hundred and thirty years.

41 And it came to pass at the end of the four hundred and thirty years, even the selfsame day it came to pass, that all the hosts of the LORD went out from the land of Egypt.

 24 *Acts 2:1–21* tells the very surprising story of what happened on one Day of Pentecost.

1 And when the day of Pentecost was fully come, they were all with one accord in one place.

2 And suddenly there came a sound from heaven as of a rushing mighty wind, and it filled all the house where they were sitting.

3 And there appeared unto them cloven tongues like as of fire, and it sat upon each of them.

4 And they were all filled with the Holy Ghost, and began to speak with other tongues, as the Spirit gave them utterance.

33 And the Egyptians were urgent upon the people, that they might send them out of the land in haste; for they said, We be all dead men.

34 And the people took their dough before it was leavened, their kneading troughs being bound up in their clothes upon their shoulders.

35 And the children of Israel did according to the word of Moses; and they borrowed of the Egyptians jewels of silver, and jewels of gold, and raiment:

36 And the LORD gave the people favour in the sight of the Egyptians, so that they lent unto them such things as they required. And they spoiled the Egyptians.

37 And the children of Israel journeyed from Rameses to Succoth, about six hundred thousand on foot that were men, beside children.

38 And a mixed multitude went up also with them; and flocks, and herds, even very much cattle.

39 And they baked unleavened cakes of the dough which they brought forth out of Egypt, for it was not leavened; because

when he smote the Egyptians, and delivered our houses. And the people bowed the head and worshipped.

28 And the children of Israel went away, and did as the LORD had commanded Moses and Aaron, so did they.

29 And it came to pass, that at midnight the LORD smote all the firstborn in the land of Egypt, from the firstborn of Pharaoh that sat on his throne unto the firstborn of the captive that was in the dungeon; and all the firstborn of cattle.

30 And Pharaoh rose up in the night, he, and all his servants, and all the Egyptians; and there was a great cry in Egypt; for there was not a house where there was not one dead.

31 And he called for Moses and Aaron by night, and said, Rise up, and get you forth from among my people, both ye and the children of Israel; and go, serve the LORD, as ye have said.

32 Also take your flocks and your herds, as ye have said, and be gone; and bless me also.

days of Elias, when the heaven was shut up three years and six months, when great famine was throughout all the land,

26 But unto none of them was Elias sent, save unto Sarepta, a city of Sidon, unto a woman that was a widow.

27 And many lepers were in Israel in the time of Eliseus the prophet; and none of them was cleansed, saving Naaman the Syrian.

28 And all they in the synagogue, when they heard these things, were filled with wrath,

29 And rose up, and thrust him out of the city, and led him unto the brow of the hill whereon their city was built, that they might cast him down headlong.

30 But he passing through the midst of them went his way.

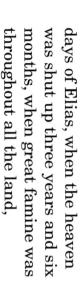 23

You can read this story in *Exodus 12:26–41.*

26 And it shall come to pass, when your children shall say unto you, What mean ye by this service?

27 That ye shall say, It is the sacrifice of the LORD's passover, who passed over the houses of the children of Israel in Egypt,

poor; he hath sent me to heal the brokenhearted, to preach deliverance to the captives, and recovering of sight to the blind, to set at liberty them that are bruised,

19 To preach the acceptable year of the Lord.

20 And he closed the book, and he gave it again to the minister, and sat down. And the eyes of all them that were in the synagogue were fastened on him.

21 And he began to say unto them, This day is this scripture fulfilled in your ears.

22 And all bare him witness, and wondered at the gracious words which proceeded out of his mouth. And they said, Is not this Joseph's son?

23 And he said unto them, Ye will surely say unto me this proverb, Physician, heal thyself: whatsoever we have heard done in Capernaum, do also here in thy country.

24 And he said, Verily I say unto you, No prophet is accepted in his own country.

25 But I tell you of a truth, many widows were in Israel in the

35 And on the morrow when he departed, he took out two pence, and gave them to the host, and said unto him, Take care of him; and whatsoever thou spendest more, when I come again, I will repay thee.

36 Which now of these three, thinkest thou, was neighbour unto him that fell among the thieves?

37 And he said, He that shewed mercy on him. Then said Jesus unto him, Go, and do thou likewise.

22 One time Jesus preached in the synagogue at Nazareth and the people didn't like what He said. Find out what they tried to do in *Luke 4:16–30.*

16 And he came to Nazareth, where he had been brought up: and, as his custom was, he went into the synagogue on the sabbath day, and stood up for to read.

17 And there was delivered unto him the book of the prophet Esaias. And when he had opened the book, he found the place where it was written,

18 The Spirit of the Lord is upon me, because he hath anointed me to preach the gospel to the

20 And thou shalt write them upon the door posts of thine house, and upon thy gates:

21 That your days may be multiplied, and the days of your children, in the land which the Lord sware unto your fathers to give them, as the days of heaven upon the earth.

21 *Luke 10:30–37*

30 And Jesus answering said, A certain man went down from Jerusalem to Jericho, and fell among thieves, which stripped him of his raiment, and wounded him, and departed, leaving him half dead.

31 And by chance there came down a certain priest that way: and when he saw him, he passed by on the other side.

32 And likewise a Levite, when he was at the place, came and looked on him, and passed by on the other side.

33 But a certain Samaritan, as he journeyed, came where he was: and when he saw him, he had compassion on him,

34 And went to him, and bound up his wounds, pouring in oil and wine, and set him on his own beast, and brought him to an inn, and took care of him.

14 That I will give you the rain of your land in his due season, the first rain and the latter rain, that thou mayest gather in thy corn, and thy wine, and thine oil.

15 And I will send grass in thy fields for thy cattle, that thou mayest eat and be full.

16 Take heed to yourselves, that your heart be not deceived, and ye turn aside, and serve other gods, and worship them;

17 And then the LORD's wrath be kindled against you, and he shut up the heaven, that there be no

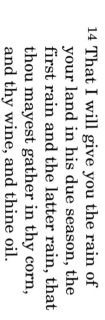

rain, and that the land yield not her fruit; and lest ye perish quickly from off the good land which the LORD giveth you.

18 Therefore shall ye lay up these my words in your heart and in your soul, and bind them for a sign upon your hand, that they may be as frontlets between your eyes.

19 And ye shall teach them your children, speaking of them when thou sittest in thine house, and when thou walkest by the way, when thou liest down, and when thou risest up.

47 And all this assembly shall know that the LORD saveth not with sword and spear: for the battle is the LORD's, and he will give you into our hands.

48 And it came to pass, when the Philistine arose, and came, and drew nigh to meet David, that David hastened, and ran toward the army to meet the Philistine.

49 And David put his hand in his bag, and took thence a stone, and slang it, and smote the Philistine in his forehead, that the stone sunk into his forehead; and he fell upon his face to the earth.

50 So David prevailed over the Philistine with a sling and with a stone, and smote the Philistine, and slew him; but there was no sword in the hand of David.

 20

These are some of the verses they had to learn: *Deuteronomy 11:13–21.*

13 And it shall come to pass, if ye shall hearken diligently unto my commandments which I command you this day, to love the LORD your God, and to serve him with all your heart and with all your soul,

man that bare the shield went before him.

42 And when the Philistine looked about, and saw David, he disdained him: for he was but a youth, and ruddy, and of a fair countenance.

43 And the Philistine said unto David, Am I a dog, that thou comest to me with staves? And the Philistine cursed David by his gods.

44 And the Philistine said to David, Come to me, and I will give thy flesh unto the fowls of the air, and to the beasts of the field.

45 Then said David to the Philistine, Thou comest to me with a sword, and with a spear, and with a shield: but I come to thee in the name of the LORD of hosts, the God of the armies of Israel, whom thou hast defied.

46 This day will the LORD deliver thee into mine hand; and I will smite thee, and take thine head from thee; and I will give the carcases of the host of the Philistines this day unto the fowls of the air, and to the wild beasts of the earth; that all the earth may know that there is a God in Israel.

a well of water springing up into everlasting life.

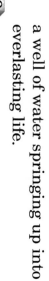

18 *Matthew 18:11–14*

11 For the Son of man is come to save that which was lost.

12 How think ye? if a man have an hundred sheep, and one of them be gone astray, doth he not leave the ninety and nine, and goeth into the mountains, and seeketh that which is gone astray?

13 And if so be that he find it, verily I say unto you, he rejoiceth more of that sheep, than of the ninety and nine which went not astray.

14 Even so it is not the will of your Father which is in heaven, that one of these little ones should perish.

19 Here is the Old Testament story of a boy who was a good shot with his sling: *1 Samuel 17:40–50.*

40 And he took his staff in his hand, and chose him five smooth stones out of the brook, and put them in a shepherd's bag which he had, even in a scrip; and his sling was in his hand: and he drew near to the Philistine.

41 And the Philistine came on and drew near unto David; and the

7 There cometh a woman of Samaria to draw water: Jesus saith unto her, Give me to drink.

8 (For his disciples were gone away unto the city to buy meat.)

9 Then saith the woman of Samaria unto him, How is it that thou, being a Jew, askest drink of me, which am a woman of Samaria? for the Jews have no dealings with the Samaritans.

10 Jesus answered and said unto her, If thou knewest the gift of God, and who it is that saith to thee, Give me to drink; thou wouldest have asked of him, and he would have given thee living water.

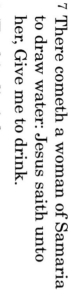

11 The woman saith unto him, Sir, thou hast nothing to draw with, and the well is deep: from whence then hast thou that living water?

12 Art thou greater than our father Jacob, which gave us the well, and drank thereof himself, and his children, and his cattle?

13 Jesus answered and said unto her, Whosoever drinketh of this water shall thirst again:

14 But whosoever drinketh of the water that I shall give him shall never thirst; but the water that I shall give him shall be in him

19 And he commanded the multitude to sit down on the grass, and took the five loaves, and the two fishes, and looking up to heaven, he blessed, and brake, and gave the loaves to his disciples, and the disciples to the multitude.

20 And they did all eat, and were filled: and they took up of the fragments that remained twelve baskets full.

21 And they that had eaten were about five thousand men, beside women and children.

 16 At His Last Supper, Jesus gave a sop to someone. You may be surprised to know who it was: *John 13:26.*

26 Jesus answered, He it is, to whom I shall give a sop, when I have dipped it. And when he had dipped the sop, he gave it to Judas Iscariot, the son of Simon.

17 Once Jesus wanted a drink but had no bucket or rope. Find out whom He asked to help Him in *John 4:6–14.*

6 Now Jacob's well was there. Jesus therefore, being wearied with his journey, sat thus on the well: and it was about the sixth hour.

ran, and fell on his neck, and kissed him.

21 And the son said unto him, Father, I have sinned against heaven, and in thy sight, and am no more worthy to be called thy son.

22 But the father said to his servants, Bring forth the best robe, and put it on him; and put a ring on his hand, and shoes on his feet:

23 And bring hither the fatted calf, and kill it; and let us eat, and be merry:

24 For this my son was dead, and is alive again; he was lost, and

is found. And they began to be merry.

15 Perhaps this is what Jesus said when He blessed the loaves and fishes in *Matthew 14:16–21*. Find out what amazing thing happened to the food.

16 But Jesus said unto them, They need not depart; give ye them to eat.

17 And they say unto him, We have here but five loaves, and two fishes.

18 He said, Bring them hither to me.

13 And not many days after the younger son gathered all together, and took his journey into a far country, and there wasted his substance with riotous living.

14 And when he had spent all, there arose a mighty famine in that land; and he began to be in want.

15 And he went and joined himself to a citizen of that country; and he sent him into his fields to feed swine.

16 And he would fain have filled his belly with the husks that the swine did eat: and no man gave unto him.

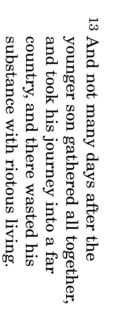

17 And when he came to himself, he said, How many hired servants of my father's have bread enough and to spare, and I perish with hunger!

18 I will arise and go to my father, and will say unto him, Father, I have sinned against heaven, and before thee,

19 And am no more worthy to be called thy son: make me as one of thy hired servants.

20 And he arose, and came to his father. But when he was yet a great way off, his father saw him, and had compassion, and

3 Then he said, Go, borrow thee vessels abroad of all thy neighbours, even empty vessels; borrow not a few.

4 And when thou art come in, thou shalt shut the door upon thee and upon thy sons, and shalt pour out into all those vessels, and thou shalt set aside that which is full.

5 So she went from him, and shut the door upon her and upon her sons, who brought the vessels to her; and she poured out.

6 And it came to pass, when the vessels were full, that she said unto her son, Bring me yet a vessel. And he said unto her, There is not a vessel more. And the oil stayed.

7 Then she came and told the man of God. And he said, Go, sell the oil, and pay thy debt, and live thou and thy children of the rest.

14

A fatted calf was eaten at this happy celebration: *Luke 15:12–24.*

12 And the younger of them said to his father, Father, give me the portion of goods that falleth to me. And he divided unto them his living.

4 Then saith one of his disciples, Judas Iscariot, Simon's son, which should betray him,

5 Why was not this ointment sold for three hundred pence, and given to the poor?

6 This he said, not that he cared for the poor; but because he was a thief, and had the bag, and bare what was put therein.

7 Then said Jesus, Let her alone: against the day of my burying hath she kept this.

8 For the poor always ye have with you; but me ye have not always.

13 Read an Old Testament story about a pot of oil that never ran out: *2 Kings 4:1–7.*

1 Now there cried a certain woman of the wives of the sons of the prophets unto Elisha, saying, Thy servant my husband is dead; and thou knowest that thy servant did fear the LORD: and the creditor is come to take unto him my two sons to be bondmen.

2 And Elisha said unto her, What shall I do for thee? tell me, what hast thou in the house? And she said, Thine handmaid hath not any thing in the house, save a pot of oil.

the field, how they grow; they toil not, neither do they spin:

29 And yet I say unto you, That even Solomon in all his glory was not arrayed like one of these.

30 Wherefore, if God so clothe the grass of the field, which to day is, and to morrow is cast into the oven, shall he not much more clothe you, O ye of little faith?

11 The Bible tells how to be beautiful on the inside: *1 Peter 3:3–4.* (*Plaiting* means braiding.)

3 Whose adorning let it not be that outward adorning of plaiting the hair, and of wearing of gold, or of putting on of apparel;

4 But let it be the hidden man of the heart, in that which is not corruptible, even the ornament of a meek and quiet spirit, which is in the sight of God of great price.

12 Some said Mary wasted the expensive perfume. What do you think? *John 12:3–8.*

3 Then took Mary a pound of ointment of spikenard, very costly, and anointed the feet of Jesus, and wiped his feet with her hair: and the house was filled with the odour of the ointment.

thy manservant, nor thy maidservant, nor thy cattle, nor thy stranger that is within thy gates:

11 For in six days the LORD made heaven and earth, the sea, and all that in them is, and rested the seventh day: wherefore the LORD blessed the sabbath day, and hallowed it.

12 Honour thy father and thy mother: that thy days may be long upon the land which the LORD thy God giveth thee.

13 Thou shalt not kill.

14 Thou shalt not commit adultery.

15 Thou shalt not steal.

16 Thou shalt not bear false witness against thy neighbour.

17 Thou shalt not covet thy neighbour's house, thou shalt not covet thy neighbour's wife, nor his manservant, nor his maidservant, nor his ox, nor his ass, nor any thing that is thy neighbour's.

10

Jesus said we should not worry about having enough clothes to wear. Why? Read *Matthew 6:28–30*.

28 And why take ye thought for raiment? Consider the lilies of

3 Thou shalt have no other gods before me.

4 Thou shalt not make unto thee any graven image, or any likeness of any thing that is in heaven above, or that is in the earth beneath, or that is in the water under the earth.

5 Thou shalt not bow down thyself to them, nor serve them: for I the Lord thy God am a jealous God, visiting the iniquity of the fathers upon the children unto the third and fourth generation of them that hate me;

6 And shewing mercy unto thousands of them that love me, and keep my commandments.

7 Thou shalt not take the name of the Lord thy God in vain; for the Lord will not hold him guiltless that taketh his name in vain.

8 Remember the sabbath day, to keep it holy.

9 Six days shalt thou labour, and do all thy work:

10 But the seventh day is the sabbath of the Lord thy God: in it thou shalt not do any work, thou, nor thy son, nor thy daughter,

4 As for me, behold, my covenant is with thee, and thou shalt be a father of many nations.

5 Neither shall thy name any more be called Abram, but thy name shall be Abraham; for a father of many nations have I made thee.

6 And I will make thee exceeding fruitful, and I will make nations of thee, and kings shall come out of thee.

7 And I will establish my covenant between me and thee and thy seed after thee in their generations for an everlasting covenant, to be a God unto thee, and to thy seed after thee.

8 And I will give unto thee, and to thy seed after thee, the land wherein thou art a stranger, all the land of Canaan, for an everlasting possession; and I will be their God.

9

In *Exodus 20:1–17* you can read about how God gave His commandments to Moses.

1 And God spake all these words, saying,

2 I am the LORD thy God, which have brought thee out of the land of Egypt, out of the house of bondage.

12 And this shall be a sign unto you; Ye shall find the babe wrapped in swaddling clothes, lying in a manger.

13 And suddenly there was with the angel a multitude of the heavenly host praising God, and saying,

14 Glory to God in the highest, and on earth peace, good will toward men.

15 And it came to pass, as the angels were gone away from them into heaven, the shepherds said one to another, Let us now go even unto Bethlehem, and see this thing which is come to pass, which the Lord hath made known unto us.

16 And they came with haste, and found Mary, and Joseph, and the babe lying in a manger.

8 Read what God said to Abraham in *Genesis 17:1–8*.

1 And when Abram was ninety years old and nine, the Lᴏʀᴅ appeared to Abram, and said unto him, I am the Almighty God; walk before me, and be thou perfect.

2 And I will make my covenant between me and thee, and will multiply thee exceedingly.

3 And Abram fell on his face: and God talked with him, saying,

135

the city of David, which is called Bethlehem; (because he was of the house and lineage of David:)

5 To be taxed with Mary his espoused wife, being great with child.

6 And so it was, that, while they were there, the days were accomplished that she should be delivered.

7 And she brought forth her firstborn son, and wrapped him in swaddling clothes, and laid him in a manger; because there was no room for them in the inn.

8 And there were in the same country shepherds abiding in the field, keeping watch over their flock by night.

9 And, lo, the angel of the Lord came upon them, and the glory of the Lord shone round about them: and they were sore afraid.

10 And the angel said unto them, Fear not: for, behold, I bring you good tidings of great joy, which shall be to all people.

11 For unto you is born this day in the city of David a Saviour, which is Christ the Lord.

know that thou wilt save Israel by mine hand, as thou hast said.

38 And it was so: for he rose up early on the morrow, and thrust the fleece together, and wringed the dew out of the fleece, a bowl full of water.

39 And Gideon said unto God, Let not thine anger be hot against me, and I will speak but this once: let me prove, I pray thee, but this once with the fleece; let it now be dry only upon the fleece, and upon all the ground let there be dew.

40 And God did so that night: for it was dry upon the fleece only, and there was dew on all the ground.

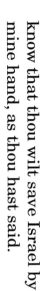

7 This is what Jesus wore after He was born. The story of His birth is in *Luke 2:1–16*.

1 And it came to pass in those days, that there went out a decree from Caesar Augustus that all the world should be taxed.

2 (And this taxing was first made when Cyrenius was governor of Syria.)

3 And all went to be taxed, every one into his own city.

4 And Joseph also went up from Galilee, out of the city of Nazareth, into Judaea, unto

5 These were the verses: *Deuteronomy 6:4–9.*

4 Hear, O Israel: The LORD our God is one LORD:

5 And thou shalt love the LORD thy God with all thine heart, and with all thy soul, and with all thy might.

6 And these words, which I command thee this day, shall be in thine heart:

7 And thou shalt teach them diligently unto thy children, and shalt talk of them when thou sittest in thine house, and when thou walkest by the way, and when thou liest down, and when thou risest up.

8 And thou shalt bind them for a sign upon thine hand, and they shall be as frontlets between thine eyes.

9 And thou shalt write them upon the posts of thy house, and on thy gates.

6 A man named Gideon asked God a question. God answered it with dew: *Judges 6:37–40.*

37 Behold, I will put a fleece of wool in the floor; and if the dew be on the fleece only, and it be dry upon all the earth beside, then shall I

138

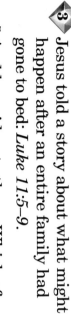

3 Jesus told a story about what might happen after an entire family had gone to bed: *Luke 11:5–9.*

5 And he said unto them, Which of you shall have a friend, and shall go unto him at midnight, and say unto him, Friend, lend me three loaves;

6 For a friend of mine in his journey is come to me, and I have nothing to set before him?

7 And he from within shall answer and say, Trouble me not: the door is now shut, and my children are with me in bed; I cannot rise and give thee.

8 I say unto you, Though he will not rise and give him, because he is his friend, yet because of his importunity he will rise and give him as many as he needeth.

9 And I say unto you, Ask, and it shall be given you; seek, and ye shall find; knock, and it shall be opened unto you.

4 Jesus said that when He comes again there will be two women doing this. See what happens to them in *Matthew 24:41.*

41 Two women shall be grinding at the mill; the one shall be taken, and the other left.

Treasures in God's Word

1

Matthew 13:45–46

45 The kingdom of heaven is like unto a merchant man, seeking goodly pearls:

46 Who, when he had found one pearl of great price, went and sold all that he had, and bought it.

2

Maybe this is the kind of floor in which the coin got lost in *Luke 15:8–10.* Notice two things the woman did to find the coin.

8 Either what woman having ten pieces of silver, if she lose one piece, doth not light a candle, and sweep the house, and seek diligently till she find it?

9 And when she hath found it, she calleth her friends and her neighbours together, saying, Rejoice with me; for I have found the piece which I had lost.

10 Likewise, I say unto you, there is joy in the presence of the angels of God over one sinner that repenteth.